32 Letters

Written by Tony & Julie Atlas

Illustrated by Jo Deng

This book is dedicated to
our children and grandchildren.

Always work hard to follow your dreams!

In 1947, Jack (Jackie) Roosevelt Robinson became the first African American Major League Baseball player when he made his debut with the Brooklyn Dodgers.

He overcame many different threats and prejudices throughout his career as the integration of baseball made many people unhappy.

He was the first among the players, but there were other firsts too.

ANGELS

Tony loved baseball. He always dreamed of
meeting the players while he listened to his
transistor radio at night while the announcers
described the plays from the game.

Tony's love for baseball continued to grow.

His dad and brother, Ken, took him to as many games as they could. Cheering their team on and eating Dodger Dogs together.

Tony played baseball every chance he could. He played on teams and with friends in the park, while his dreams continued to grow.

He wanted to be part of Major League Baseball, and the California Angels were the team closest to his home.

Tony wanted to be a batboy for the California Angels,
but he didn't know anyone on the team who could help him.

Sometimes, opportunities come from people you know.

Other times, you have to make your own opportunities,
especially when you don't know anyone who can help you.

So, he wrote a letter and put it in the mailbox.

Then, he waited.

Every day, Tony went to the mailbox to see if he had gotten a response, and every day, his answer came in the form of an empty mailbox.

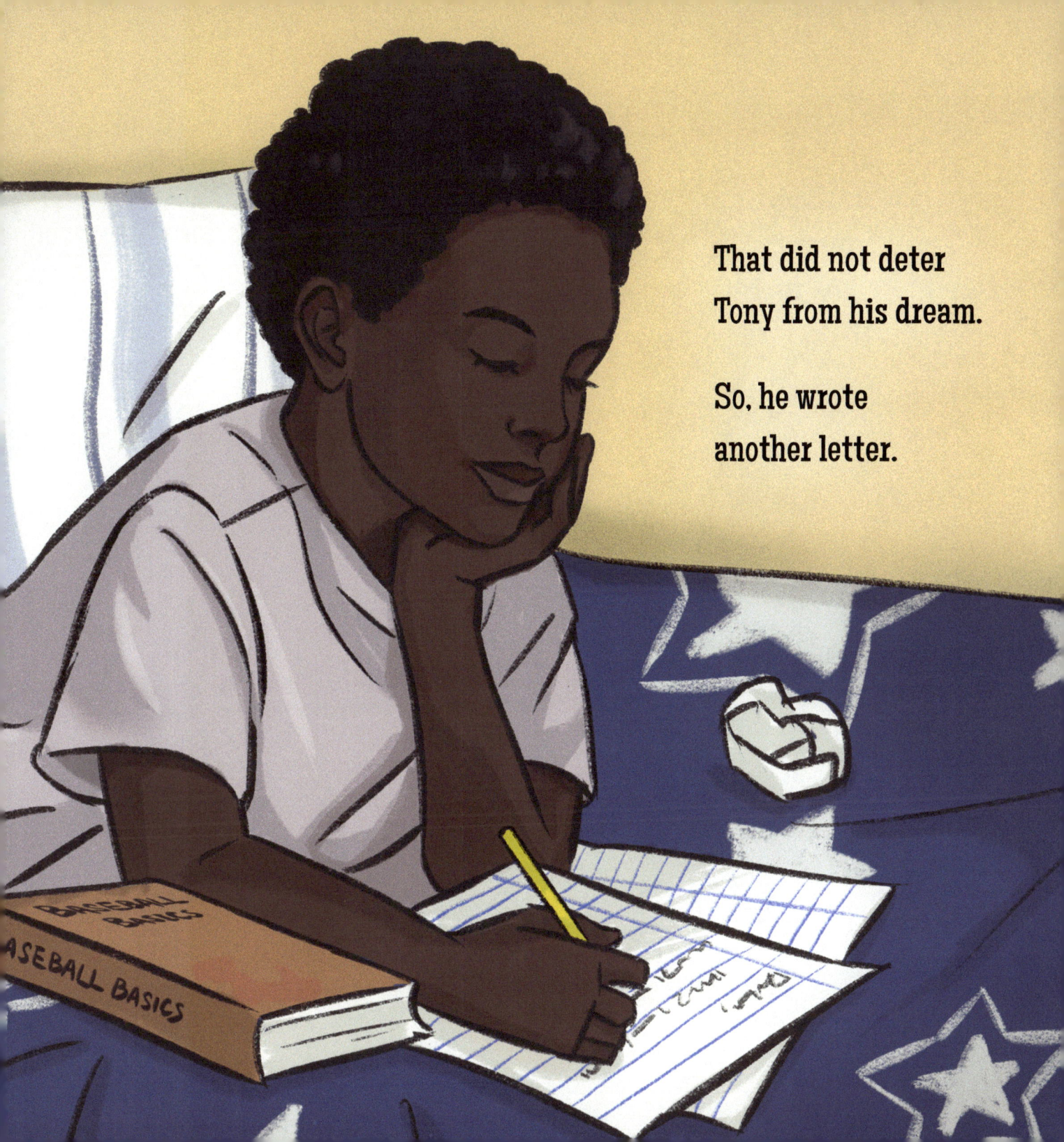

That did not deter
Tony from his dream.

So, he wrote
another letter.

After many weeks of writing unanswered letters,
Tony knew he had to do something more.

So, he attached a copy of his report card in his letter to show
that he was a hard-working and successful student in school.

Still, he did not get a response.

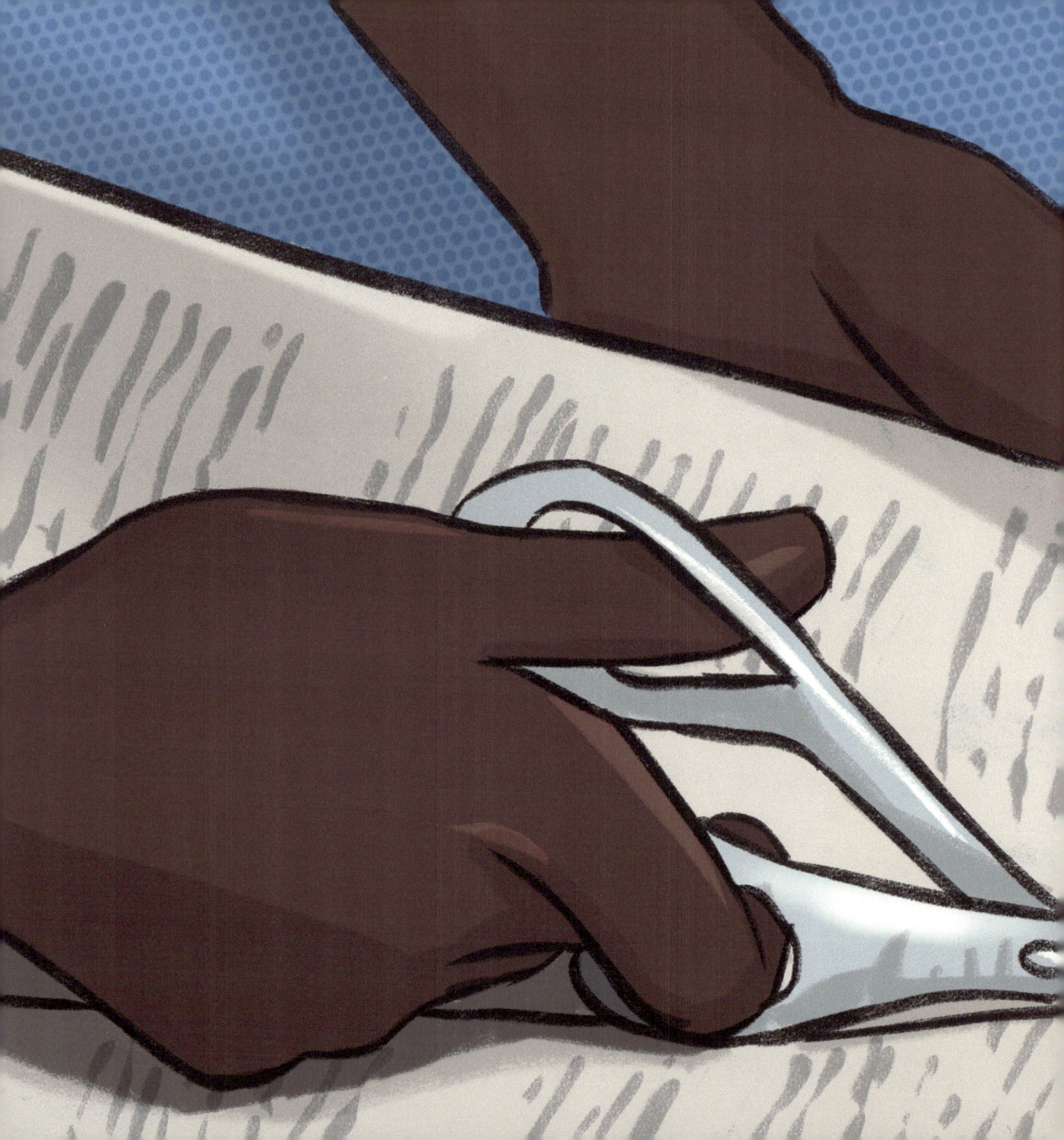

Then the newspaper featured him as the Newspaper Carrier of the week, so he sent a copy of that article in his next letter to the Angels.

Still, he did not get a response.

Tony wrote about the award he won for finishing second place for Community Service from the Junior Optimist Club International.

Dear LA Ang

Still, he did not get a response.

Every week, he wrote a new letter. Then, he waited for a reply.

Nothing would deter Tony from following his dream of becoming a batboy.

He wrote letters week after week.

The weeks turned into months,
and the months turned into seasons.

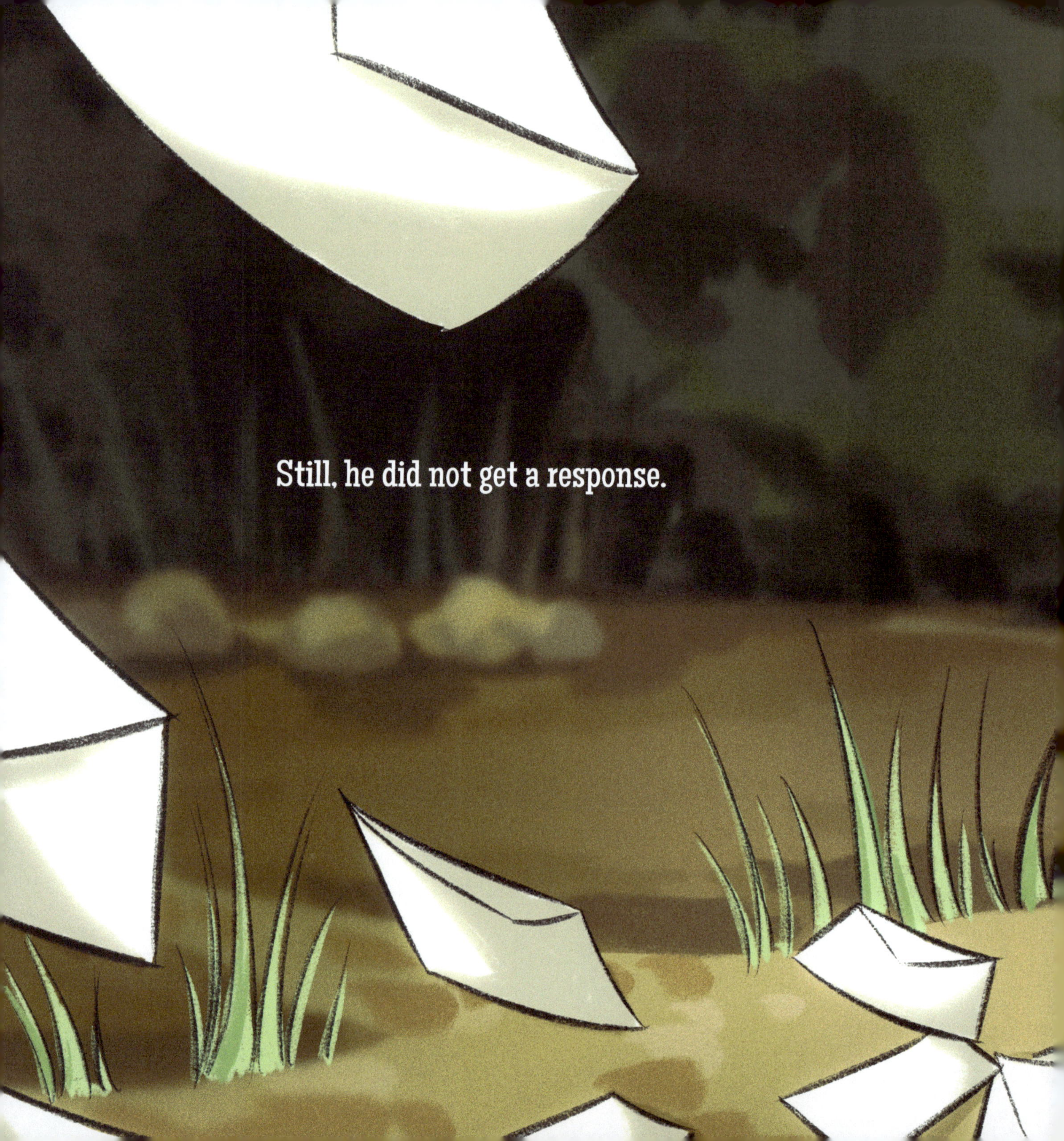

Still, he did not get a response.

Tony wrote 32 letters
to the Angels.

He wrote a letter almost
every week for most of 1977.

Tony's persistence finally paid off.

Dave Howells, the visiting clubhouse manager, called him and invited him to work as a part-time batboy during the 1977 season.

Tony's efforts stood out, and he was hired as a full-time batboy in the visiting clubhouse for the 1978 season.

Tony had done what no one who looked like him had done before, he became the first full-time African-American batboy for the California Angels.

The California Angels, now called the Los Angeles Angels, decided to allow him to be part of their team.

Even though Tony is not a batboy anymore, he still loves baseball. Although, these days, he watches the games on TV or streams them on his phone or computer instead of listening to them on his transistor radio.

And, of course, he stays in contact with the friends he met in Major League Baseball.

Anthony K. Atlas, Sr. (Tony), was born in Riverside, California, to Chester and Virginia Atlas. He has seven siblings, Phyllis, Robert, Rose, Kenneth, Michelle, Kimberly, and Christopher.

His education includes a Bachelor's Degree in Sociology from California State University, Fullerton, a Master's Degree in Sports Administration from the American Military University and a Master's Degree in Strategic Studies from the United States Army War College.

Tony is married to his wife, Julie. They have three adult children, Corrine, Anthony II, and Lara. They also have four grandchildren and four honorary daughters, Jo, Maddy, Paula and Janeva.

Tony spent 15 years as a law enforcement officer and 26 years in the Army, rising to the rank of Colonel. He is an avid sports fan, especially baseball and his beloved Los Angeles Dodgers.

Tony is retired from the U.S. Army and resides in the Richmond, Virginia area.

www.ingramcontent.com/pod-product-compliance
Lightning Source LLC
Chambersburg PA
CBHW041429090426
42741CB00003B/99

9798218064907